Mamma mia!

Benny Anders...

6

Super-Trouper

Words and music by
Benny Andersson, Stig Anderson & Björn Ulvaeus

Lyrics in the score:

I was sick and tired of ev-'ry-thing when I called___ you last night from
Fa-cing twen-ty thou-sand of your friends how can a-ny-one be so

Glas - gow. All I do is eat and sleep and sing, wish-ing ev-
lone - ly? Part of a suc-cess that ne-ver ends, still I'm think-

the last show. So i-ma-gine I was
you on - ly. There are mo-ments when I

- 'ry show was the last___ show. oo_____
- ing a-bout you on - ly. you on - ly.

the last show. oo_____
you on - ly.

14

Money, money, money

Words and music by
Benny Andersson, Stig Anderson & Björn Ulvaeus